Ukulele Primer

For Beginners

Book with Online Video Access

By
Bert Casey

For Soprano, Concert, & Tenor Ukuleles
C Tuning (G, C, E, A)

Free Online Video Access
Go to this address on the internet:
cvls.com/extras/ukulele/

If you encounter any issues with these files, please email us at
sales@cvls.com

Introduction

The *Ukulele Primer Book with Online Video Access* will quickly transform you from an absolute beginner into a ukulele player with a full understanding of the fundamentals and techniques of playing and having fun with the uke. This clear, step-by-step method includes many photographs, large easy to read music notation, and an easy to understand sequence of learning that has been meticulously developed and tested over a 25 year period. With each new song, you'll learn new techniques to establish a firm foundation that will enable you to enjoy playing ukulele for many years.

This book also contains the lyrics and melody lines to each of the songs so that you can start playing and singing immediately. Each song is played at two different speeds on the Video, a slow speed for learning the song and practicing, and a performance speed where the song is played and sung with all of the verses.

The Author

Bert Casey, the author of this book, has been a professional performer and teacher in the Atlanta area for over 30 years. Bert plays several instruments (acoustic guitar, electric guitar, bass guitar, mandolin, banjo, ukulele, and flute) and has written seven instructional courses (*Acoustic Guitar Primer, Acoustic Guitar Book 2, Electric Guitar Primer, Bass Guitar Primer, Mandolin Primer, Flatpicking Guitar Songs, Ukulele Primer,* and *Bluegrass Fakebook*). Bert performed for several years in Atlanta and the Southeast with his bands Home Remedy and Blue Moon. His talent and willingness to share have helped thousands of students learn and experience the joy of playing a musical instrument.

Brief History of the Ukulele

The ukulele dates back to 1879 when Portugese immigrant workers arrived in Honolulu aboard the English ship Ravenscrag. They brought with them a small guitar like instrument called the machete, which immediately became popular with the native Hawaiians. It was renamed ukulele or "jumping flea" because of the way a player's fingers jumped around the fretboard. The ardent support of King David Kalakaua helped establish the ukulele or uke in Hawaiian music and culture.

The ukulele was introduced to the mainland USA at the Pacific-Panama Exposition in San Francisco in 1915. The Hawaiian Pavilion featured a guitar and ukulele ensemble that helped spark a fad for Hawaiian-themed songs among Tin Pan Alley songwriters. The ukulele soon became an icon of the Jazz Age and American instrument makers soon followed with their own ukulele models. Uke players Roy Smeck and Cliff Edwards (Ukulele Ike) were pop stars of their era. Laurel & Hardy often used ukuleles and George Formby popularized the banjo uke in England.

The Great Depression and World War II slowed the interest in the uke, but in the 40's & 50's, Arthur Godrey played the baritone uke on radio shows and television and sparked a revival. In 1968 Tiny Tim performed his version of *Tiptoe Through The Tulips* on numerous TV appearances.

The current wave of uke popularity can be traced to George Harrison of the Beatles, who was a big fan of the ukulele. Paul McCartney, Elvis Costello, Jack Johnson, and Brian May have also performed with the uke. Israel Kamakawiwo'ole had a big uke hit with his medley of *Somewhere Over the Rainbow* and *What A Wonderful World*. Current stars like Jake Shimabukuro have shown that there are no limits with the music that can be played on the ukulele.

Other Ukulele Products

The following ukulele products are also available from Watch & Learn, Inc. to help with your further enjoyment of the instrument.

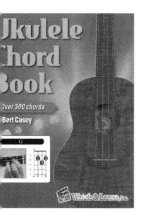

The *Ukulele Chord Book* is a reference book with over 300 chords with photos to clearly illustrate how to play each chord. The accompanying diagram displays proper fret position, fingering, and labels the notes of the chord. This extensive chord chart shows 12 common chord types in two different neck positions in all twelve major keys. It also includes sections on Moveable Chords, Common Chords in Each Major Key, and a full neck diagram of the ukulele with all notes labeled. This handy book will help you to advance your ukulele playing to the next level by giving you more variety in your chord voicings.

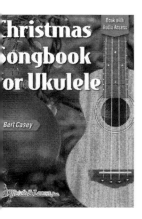

The *Christmas Songbook for Ukulele* with Online Audio Access features beginner to intermediate arrangements for classic Christmas songs. Each song features detailed strum patterns, chord charts, lyrics, and vocal melody notation. The songs were arranged so that you can play the rhythm part while singing along. The second portion of this book displays each song along with extended lyrics and chord progressions. This is a great setup for sing-alongs because the lyrics are written in a large font so that multiple singers and musicians can read along. This course also includes online access to audio tracks to help you learn and practice.

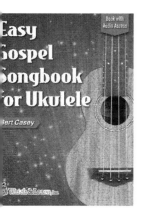

The *Easy Gospel Songbook for Ukulele* with Online Audio Access features beginner to intermediate arrangements for classic gospel songs. Each song features detailed strum patterns, chord charts, lyrics, and vocal melody notation. The songs were arranged so that you can play the rhythm part while singing along. The second portion of this book displays each song along with extended lyrics and chord progressions. This is a great setup for sing-alongs because the lyrics are written in a large font so that multiple singers and musicians can read along. This course also includes online access to audio tracks to help you learn and practice.

These products are available on Amazon.com. If you have any questions, problems, or comments, please contact us at:

Watch & Learn, Inc.
2947 East Point St.
East Point, GA 30344
800-416-7088
sales@cvls.com

Table Of Contents

Appendix

Section 1
Getting Started

You can watch the video at this address on the internet:

cvls.com/extras/ukulele/

If you encounter any issues with these files, please email us at
sales@cvls.com

The Ukulele

There are four main types of ukuleles as shown by the photos below. This course will work with the Soprano, Concert, and Tenor ukes, all tuned G C E A.

The baritone ukulele is usually tuned like the first four strings of a guitar (D G B E) and will not be used in this course. I'll be using a tenor ukulele primarily, but you could use a soprano or concert uke with this course.

Soprano   Concert   Tenor   Baritone

Take your ukulele to your local music store to make sure it is in good playing condition and has good strings. If it needs any repairs, they can probably do it on the spot.

TIP *Get to know the folks at your local music store. They can be a great help with supplies, lessons, & advice.*

Parts of the Ukulele

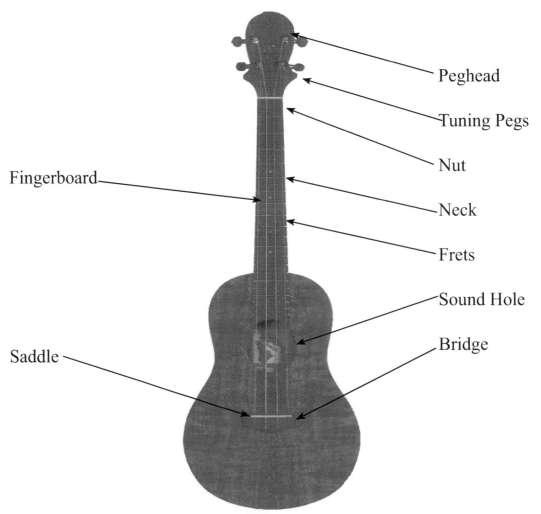

Peghead

Tuning Pegs

Nut

Fingerboard

Neck

Frets

Sound Hole

Bridge

Saddle

If you need to buy a ukulele, it is usually safer to purchase your first instrument from a reputable music store, who will make sure that the instrument is adjusted properly and offer service after the sale. Resist the temptation to buy a cheap plastic uke. These are little more than toys and can be very hard to play. You should purchase a case for your ukulele because many are broken by accident. There are several types of cases to pick from. You may buy a hard shell, which is most durable, a soft shell, or a gig bag. A case should keep the ukulele dry and protected when being transported.

Your ukulele should be stored in a neutral environment. This means not too cold, not too hot, not too wet, and not too dry. The wood in a ukulele is subject to change and will expand or contract in response to it's environment. Too much of any of these conditions could cause permanent damage. For example, never leave your uke in your car for long periods of time during summer or winter months. Attics and basements tend to be poor locations for storing a ukulele as well.

TIP *Always use a case or gig bag when transporting your instrument from one place to another.*

Tuning

There are several popular tunings for the ukulele. The two most common are the C tuning (G, C, E, A) and the A tuning (A, D, F♯, B) with the C tuning being the most popular.

This course will use a soprano, concert, or tenor ukulele tuned to a C tuning (G C E A). Tune the four strings of the ukulele to the same pitch as the four notes shown on the piano in the following diagrams.

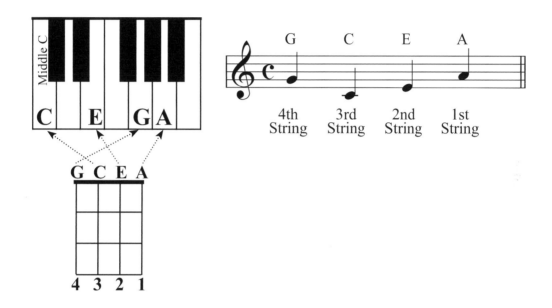

Video

Listen to the tuning section on the Video to learn how to tune your ukulele so you will be in tune with the exercises and songs when you play along.

Electronic Tuner

An electronic tuner is the fastest and most accurate way to tune a ukulele. I highly recommend getting one. It may take months or years for a beginner to develop the skills to tune a uke correctly by ear. The electronic tuner is more precise and is used by virtually every professional player.

TIP *Never leave your instrument in a car or trunk during extreme heat or cold.*

Holding the Ukulele

Many ukulele players are self taught and have developed their own unique style and methods of playing. There is no one correct way to play the uke. I'll be showing you the most common techniques to use and the ones that I use.

At first you will be holding the ukulele sitting down. Use a straight back chair or stool so you can sit with good posture and have free arm movement without banging the uke on your arms or the furniture.

Sit erect with both feet on the floor. The ukulele should be braced against your chest with your right forearm so the neck doesn't move when you change hand positions. Press lightly with the right forearm to press the uke against your ribs. The left hand is used for balance.

The standing position is harder and takes a little more getting used to. Again, press the uke against your right side with your right forearm. You can use a ukulele strap if you like.

Always keep an extra set of strings in your case.
You never know when you will break one.

4

Left Hand Position

Arm Position

The left elbow should hang freely to the outside of the left leg. Make sure you aren't resting the left elbow on your leg. This will avoid undue stress on the elbow and wrist.

Thumb Position

You will see different players use different thumb positions, but I prefer this position because it allows you to play all of the chords without having to change your thumb position (Figure A).

The pad of your left thumb should be positioned on the center of the back of the ukulele neck. This will be our core position (Figure B).

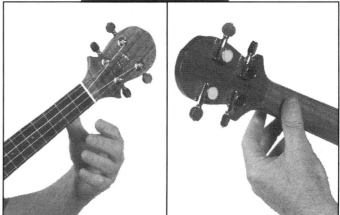

Figure A   **Figure B**

Wrist Position

The wrist should be below the ukulele neck in a comfortable position. Don't strain your wrist to one side or the other (Figure C).

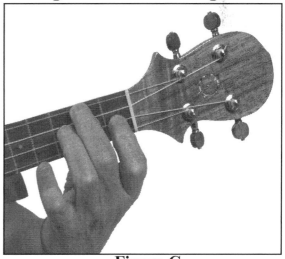

Figure C

Fingernails

You will need to keep your fingernails trimmed so that you can easily press down on the fingerboard.

Strumming

There are a variety of ways to strum the ukulele. You can use your thumb, your index finger, a felt pick, or fingerpick. I'll use the index finger for this course.

Thumb   **Index Finger**   **Felt Pick**

Index Finger Strum

Curl your right index (Figure 1). Place the thumb on the side of the first joint of the index finger (Figure 2). Strike the strings with the finger nail of your right index finger (Figure 3).

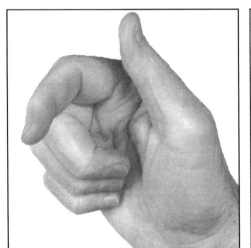

Figure 1

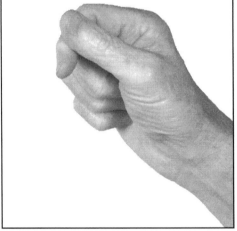

Figure 2

Figure 3

Right Hand Position

Position your right hand so that you strike the strings in the center of the sound hole. Don't brace your right hand on the ukulele. It should move freely with no part of the hand or wrist touching the ukulele. You should be moving from your wrist and not the elbow.

Our First Chord

The C Chord

The first chord we'll learn is a C chord. Place the ring finger of your left hand on the 1st string at the 3rd fret.

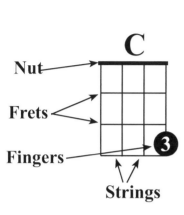

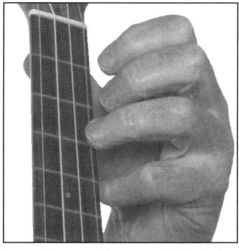

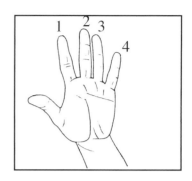

Strum down on all four strings with your right index finger and listen to each string to make sure you are getting a clear sound. Play along with the Video.

C - C - C - C - C - C - C - C - C - C - C - C - C - C - C - C - C - C

Check the following to make sure you are using good technique:

1. The pad of the thumb should be placed on the center of the ukulele neck (check the photos on page 5.
2. The fingers should be arched so that the tips of the fingers fret the strings. Do not touch an adjacent string with one of your fingers. Check the following photo for the correct position.

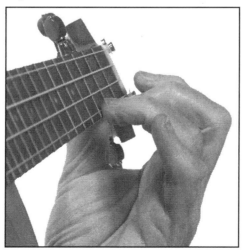

Practicing a little each day is better than practicing a lot all at once.

7

Ukulele Notation

The ukulele notation in this book is written on two lines or staves. The top staff is the melody line with lyrics. The bottom line is the strumming pattern for the right hand.

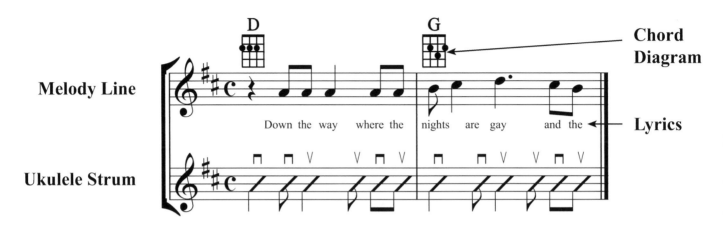

The exercises contain only one line or staff. This is the ukulele strumming notation.

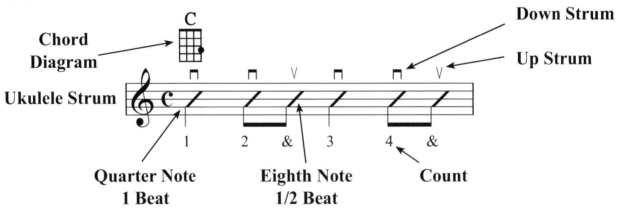

Ukulele Tablature

Starting on page 40, we use ukulele tablature or tab. Tablature is a system for writing music using numbers that shows the proper string and fret to play.

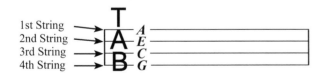

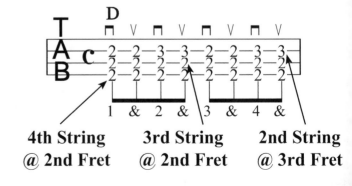

Practice new songs slowly and relaxed. Work on speed after you can play it perfectly.

Section 2
Playing Popular Songs
on the Ukulele

You can watch the video at this address on the internet:

cvls.com/extras/ukulele/

If you encounter any issues with these files, please email us at
sales@cvls.com

The G7 Chord

We learned the C chord on page 7. Our next chord is a G^7 chord. Place your fingers as shown below. Make sure to arch your fingers and use your fingertips.

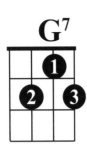

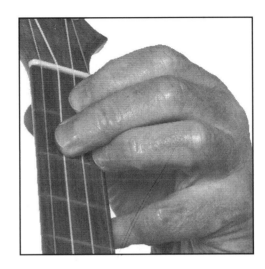

Exercise 1

Strum down on all four strings with your right index finger and listen to each string to make sure you are getting a clear sound. Play along with the Video.

$$G^7 - G^7 - G^7 - G^7 - G^7 - G^7 - G^7 - G^7 - G^7 - G^7 - G^7 - G^7$$

Changing Chords

Now we'll work on changing chords smoothly and easily. An essential technique that we'll use is called the guide finger. Be sure to watch the Video in this section because it shows the correct movement of the left hand and fingers.

GUIDE FINGERS

A guide finger remains on the same string, but then must slide from one fret to another. There are several advantages to using guide fingers.

1. Since the finger is already on the correct string, it'll cut down on mistakes.
2. Sliding from one fret to another creates a pleasing chord changing sound and cuts down on the time it takes to change chords.
3. It allows you to stay in contact with the ukulele making it easier to develop a sense of feel.

Exercise 2

Practice changing from the C chord to the G^7 chord using the left ring finger as a guide finger. Strum down once on each chord. Go back and forth with this chord change until it is comfortable. Make sure to play along with the Video.

$C - G^7 - C - G^7 - C - G^7 - C - G^7 - C - G^7 - C - G^7 - C - G^7 - C - G^7$

This will seem very awkward at first, but you should go through these steps to get more comfortable with the chord changes:
1. Practice the changes looking only at your left hand.
2. Next, practice looking at only your right hand.
3. Finally, practice without looking at either hand.

Learning to Strum

The right hand is the driver when playing ukulele. This hand creates most of the sound we make and is responsible for the rhythm, dynamics, and fluidity of our playing. We've already discussed basic right and left hand positions and techniques, so now let's focus on learning how to strum.

Exercise 3

Most of the songs in this course will be in 4/4 or common time. This means there are four beats per measure. Strum down smoothly and evenly on all four strings of the ukulele. Strike the strings with the nail of your right index finger. Count 1 2 3 4 very evenly and strum down each time you count. Play along with the Video.

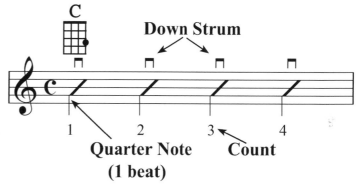

Exercise 4

Combine Exercises 2 & 3 to play one measure of the strum per chord.

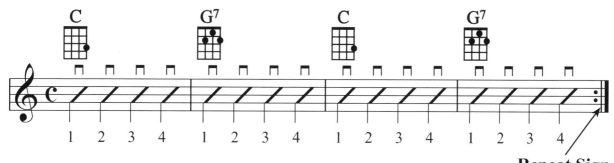

TIP
The strumming hand is the driver when playing ukulele. It's hard to make a sound without it.

11

Repeat Sign
Repeat the previous measures.

Now we'll combine the basic strum with the following chord changes. Follow the music closely and play along with the Video.

He's Got the Whole World...

Traditional

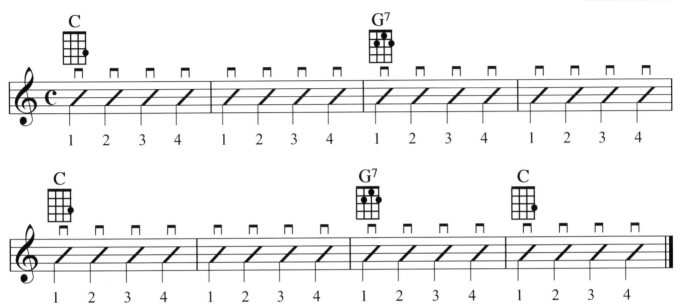

Practice this until you can play along with the Video comfortably. Repeat this section on the Video as many times as you need.

Note - Your fingertips are probably getting sore. It takes a couple of weeks of practicing every day to build up callouses on your left hand. If your hand or wrist is sore, you are pressing too hard or distorting the position of your hand and wrist. Check your left hand position with the Video.

This basic strum is a great starting point for learning how to strum. However, to make the ukulele really sound good, we need to add more variety to the right hand strumming technique. On the following pages, we'll learn constant motion.

TIP *Working with a metronome helps you practice slowly and gradually increase speed.*

Constant Motion

One of the most import concepts and techniques for strumming is constant motion. When you watch a great ukulele player, watch his right hand, especially when he's playing rhythm. The right hand will usually be in constant motion. ***The right hand acts as the metronome. The down motion is followed in time by the up motion.***

Exercise 5

Place your left hand over the strings to mute them. Playing all four strings of the uke, strum the following pattern. Strum down with the nail of your index finger and strum up with the pad of your index finger. Repeat this over and over, never stopping with the right hand. This is the secret to strumming: constant motion.

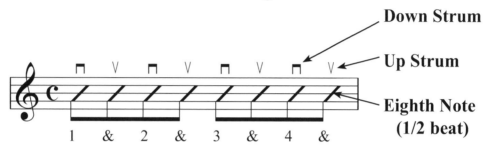

Exercise 6

Here's something a little harder. Use the same motion and count, but this time, only hit the strings on beat 1. Be sure to play along with the Video.

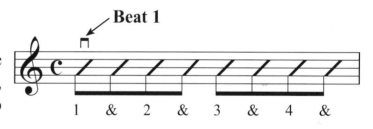

Exercise 7

This time, hit the strings on beats 1 & 3.

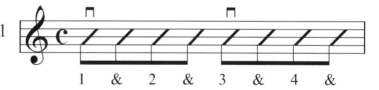

Exercise 8

Now hit the strings on all 4 beats.

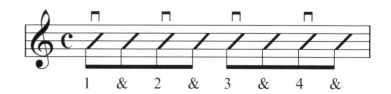

Purchase a music stand. People who use one tend to practice up to 30% longer.

Exercise 9

This is our first strumming pattern. Mute the strings with the left hand. Using constant motion and hit the strings on 1 2 & 3 4 &. This will be down, down up, down, down up. Play along with the Video.

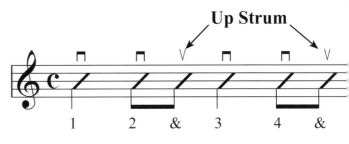

Exercise 10

Now hold down the C chord and play this strum. Again, play along with the Video.

Exercise 11

Next hold down the G⁷ chord and play this strum. Play along with the Video.

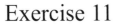

Exercise 12

Now practice the chord changes along with the strum.

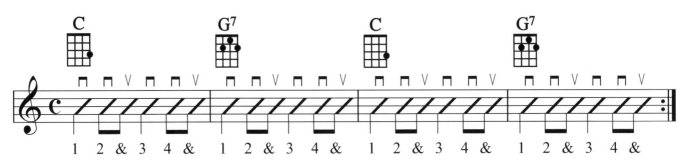

Next we'll use this strum with the C and G⁷ chords for *He's Got The Whole World In His Hands*.

Note - We will play all of the songs in this course at two or three speeds. The first speeds will be a slow practice speed. I'll talk you through the chord changes and strums and we'll play along with a metronome. The fastest speed will be a performance speed while singing the song. At first, it can be very hard to sing and play at the same time. Concentrate on the ukulele part until you are comfortable with it. Then you can try singing along. Always practice with the Video to ensure that you are using the correct technique and timing.

He's Got the Whole World...

Traditional

Key of C

He's got the whole world in His hands, He's got the whole world in His hands, He's got the whole world in His hands, He's got the whole world in His hands.

He's got my brothers and my sisters in His hands,
He's got my brothers and my sisters in His hands,
He's got my brothers and my sisters in His hands,
He's got the whole world in His hands.

He's got the sun and the rain in His hands,
He's got the moon and the stars in His hands,
He's got the wind and the clouds in His hands,
He's got the whole world in His hands.

He's got the rivers and the oceans in His hands,
He's got the rivers and the oceans in His hands,
He's got the rivers and the oceans in His hands,
He's got the whole world in His hands.

He's got everybody here in His hands,
He's got everybody here in His hands,
He's got everybody here in His hands,
He's got the whole world in His hands.

15

Exercise 13

Here's a variation on the strum we just used. Count 1 2 & 3 & 4 & and strum down, down up, down up, down up. Mute the strings with the left hand while practicing this.

Exercise 14

Now hold down the C chord with the left hand and practice this strum. Try accenting the first beat of each measure.

Then do the same thing with the G⁷ chord.

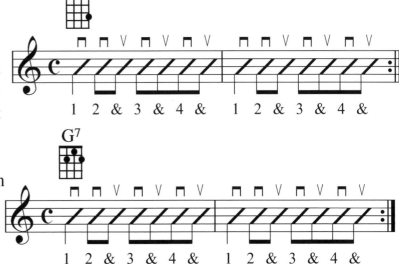

Exercise 15

Now, practice the strum with the chord changes. Make sure to use constant motion with your right hand.

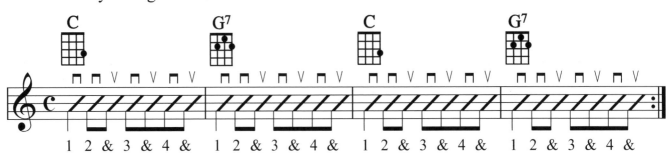

We'll use this strum in another two chord song, *Pay Me My Money Down*. Make sure to practice along with the DVD.

Note - We will be adding new strums on almost every song to make your playing more interesting and fun. If you want to play a song before mastering the new strum, you can substitute the basic strums in the first part of the course. Also, as you learn more strums, try using each strum with different songs in this course. Check page 44 for the complete strum library.

Practicing in front of a full length mirror can help you see your technique better. You'll see things you never see from your usual sight line.

16

Pay Me My Money Down

Traditional

Soon as that boat was clear of the bar
Pay me my money down
He knocked me down with the end of a spar
Pay me my money down
Chorus

If I had been a rich man's son
Pay me my money down
I'd sit on the river and watch it run
Pay me my money down
Chorus

The C⁷ Chord

The C^7 Chord

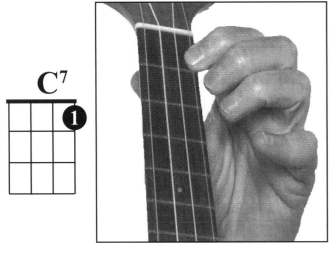

The F Chord

The F Chord

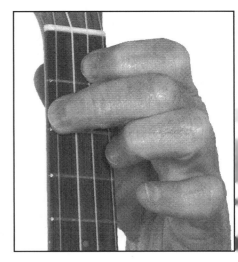

Exercise 16

Practice the chord changes, C - C^7 - F. Strum down once on each chord.

C - C^7 - F - C - C^7 - F - C - C^7 - F - C - C^7 - F - C - C^7 - F - C - C^7 - F

Exercise 17

The next song is a little faster, so we're going to change the strum a little. Count 1 2 & 3 & 4 and strum down, down up, down up, down. Play along with the Video.

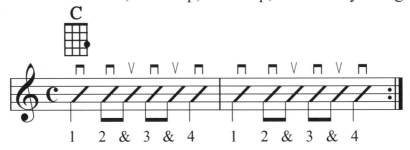

Note - Before playing a new song, you should practice the new strums with the new chord changes. Go back to Exercise 16 and play one measure of the strum per chord. As you learn each song, examine the chord changes and focus on any segments that you have problems with. Always break the hard parts into smaller segments to practice, then join them together after you can play them comfortably.

We'll use this strum along with the C, C^7, F, and G^7 chords to play our next song, *When The Saints Go Marching In*. Play along with the Video.

Record your practice occasionally and listen to it.

When the Saints Go Marching In

Traditional

Oh, when the sun refuse to shine
Oh, when the sun refuse to shine
Oh Lord, I want to be in that number
When the sun refuse to shine

Oh, when the stars have disappeared
Oh, when the stars have disappeared
Oh Lord, I want to be in that number
When the stars have disappeared

3/4 Time or Waltz Time

The next song is in 3/4 time or waltz time. This means there are three beats per measure instead of four beats per measure as in all the previous songs. Count 1 2 3, 1 2 3, 1 2 3, 1 2 3.

Exercise 18

As you count 1 2 3, 1 2 3, strum down once on each beat while holding the F chord. Accent beat 1 of each measure. Play along with the Video to get the proper timing and feel.

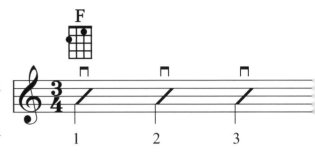

Exercise 19

To construct a more interesting strum, count 1 2 & 3 & and strum down, down up, down up. Again, play along with the Video.

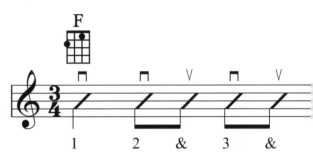

Exercise 20

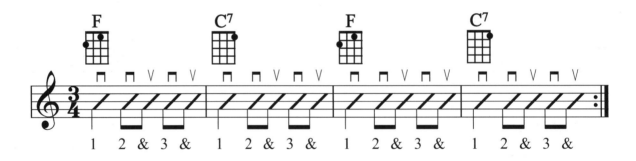

We will combine the F and C⁷ chords with the 3/4 strum to play *Streets Of Laredo*.

Streets of Laredo

Traditional

TIP *It is a good idea to have your instrument set up by your local music store at least once a year.*

The G Chord

We're switching to the key of G and learning two new chords, the G & D chords. Here's the G chord.

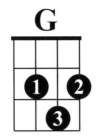

The D Chord

The D chord requires fretting the 2nd, 3rd, and 4th strings, all at the 2nd fret. Depending on the size of your fingers and hands and which type of ukulele you are using, it can be very hard to fit all of the fingers in. Try each of these chord shapes. I use the second shape, but experiment and see which is the easiest for you.

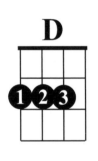

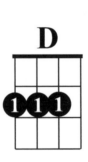

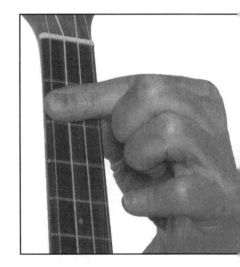

Exercise 21

Practice changing between the G & D chords. Go slowly and make sure you're getting a good clean sound on each chord.

G - D - G - D - G - D - G - D - G - D - G - G - D - G - G - D - G

Using the strum from page 16, play one measure on each chord. Play along with the Video.

Now we'll use the G and D chords to play *Tom Dooley.*

TIP

Tom Dooley

Traditional

Key of G

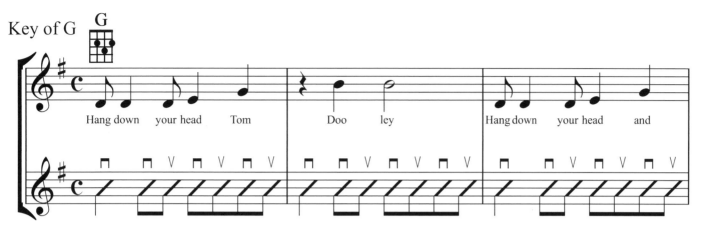

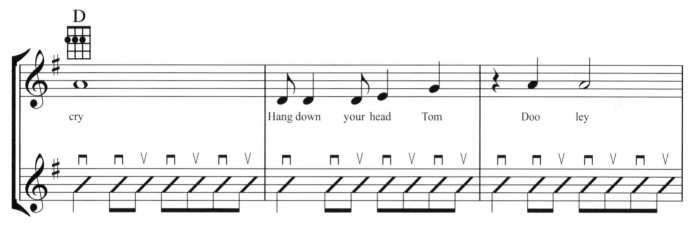

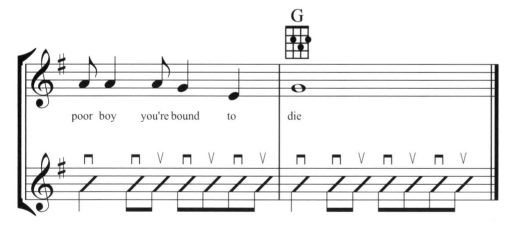

TIP *Strings should be replaced at least every three months, sometimes sooner.*

Exercise 22

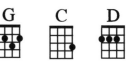

There are no new chords on the next song, but they occur in a different sequence. Practice the following chord changes.

G - C - D - G - C - D - G - C - D - G - C - D - G - C - D - G

The Muted Strum

Here's a new strum using a muted technique. Count 1 & 2 & 3 & 4 & and strum down up, down up, down up, down up. Mute the strum on beats 2 and 2& and 4 and 4&. You accomplish this be relaxing the pressure with your left thumb. Practice along with the Video to master this technique.

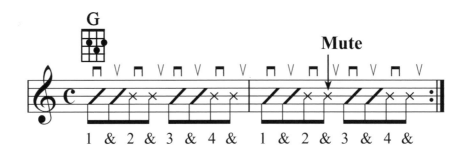

We'll use the G, C, and D chords along with the muted strum for *Worried Man Blues.*

Worried Man Blues

Traditional

The D⁷ Chord

The D⁷ chord is used as a transitional chord to change from D to G.

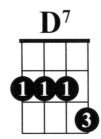

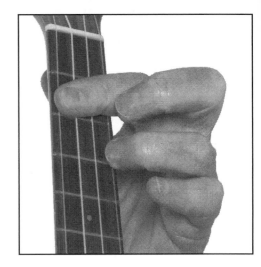

Exercise 23

Practice these chord changes.

D   D⁷   G

D - D⁷ - G - D - D⁷ - G - D - D⁷ - G - D - D⁷ - G - D - D⁷ - G - D - D⁷ - G

We'll use the G, C, D, & D⁷ chords along with the muted strum to play *Banks Of The Ohio*.

TIP *Loosen the strings on your instrument when flying or driving through high elevations.*

Banks Of The Ohio

Traditional

The A Chord

The next song is in the key of D, so we need to learn the A chord.

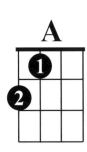

Exercise 24

Now practice changing between the D, G, and A chords.

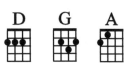

D - G - A - D - G - A - D - G - A - D - G - A - D - G - A - D - G - A - D

Note - Every time you see a new chord sequence that you have not played before, practice the chord changes until you are comfortable with them. It's always easier and more efficient to break the music into smaller segments to practice than playing all the way through the song. First master the smaller segments or exercises, then put all of the pieces together to play the song.

The Calypso Strum

We will use a Calypso type strum for the next song. Count 1 2& &4& and play down, down up, up down up. Play along with the Video to get the correct timing.

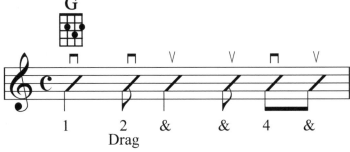

Combining the D, G, and A chords with the Calypso strum, we'll play *Jamaica Farewell.*

28

Jamaica Farewell

Sounds of laughter everywhere
And the dancing girls swaying to and fro
I must admit my heart is there
Though I've been from Maine to Mexico
Chorus

Down at the market you can hear
Ladies cry out while on their heads they bear
Akey rice, salt fish are nice,
And the rum is good any time of year
Chorus

The A⁷ Chord

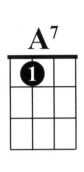

The Em Chord

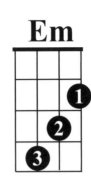

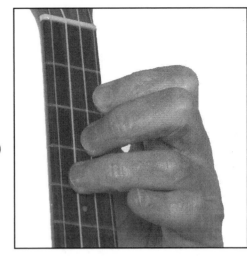

Exercise 25

Practice changing between the G, A⁷, D, and D⁷ chords.

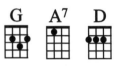

G - A⁷ - D - G - A⁷ - D - D - D⁷ - G - D - D⁷ - G -D - D⁷ - G - D - D⁷ - G

Exercise 26

Now practice changing between the G, Em, and D chords.

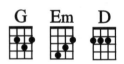

G - Em - D - G - Em - D - G - Em - D - G - Em - D - G - Em - D - G

Exercise 27

Also practice changing between the G, G⁷, & C chords.

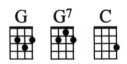

G - G⁷ - C - G - G⁷ - C - G - G⁷ - C - G - G⁷ - C - G - G⁷ - C - G - G⁷ - C

Combine the G, G⁷, C, A⁷, D, D⁷, and Em chords with the 3/4 strum we learned earlier (page 20) to play *Amazing Grace*.

TIP *A good ukulele teacher can speed up your improvement by 200 to 300 percent.*

Amazing Grace

Traditional

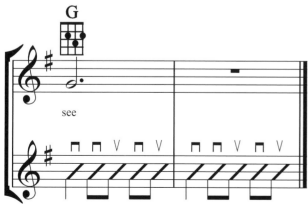

Twas grace that taught my heart to fear
And grace my fears relieved
How precious did that grace appear
The hour I first believed

When we've been here ten thousand years
Bright shining as the sun
We've no less days to sing God's praise
Than when we've first begun

The B♭ Chord

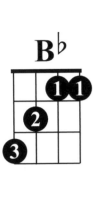

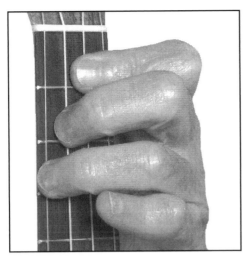

The F⁷ Chord

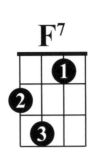

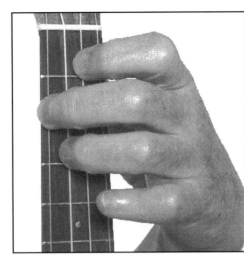

Exercise 28

Practice changing between the F and B♭ chords.

F - B♭ - F - B♭ - F - B♭ - F - B♭ - F - B♭ - F - B♭ - F - B♭ - F - B♭ - F

F - F⁷ - B♭ - F - F⁷ - B♭ - F - F⁷ - B♭ - F - F⁷ - B♭ - F - F⁷ - B♭

Exercise 29

Here's a two measure strum combing two strums we learned earlier.

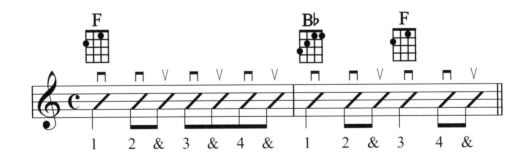

Use the F, F⁷, B♭, and C chords along with the strum to play *Swing Low, Sweet Chariot.*

TIP *If you're going to stand when performing, you should practice while standing.*

32

Swing Low, Sweet Chariot

Traditional

The B♭m⁶ Chord

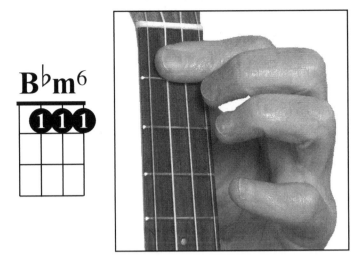

Exercise 30

Practice changing from B♭ to B♭m⁶.

B♭ - B♭m⁶ - F - B♭ - B♭m⁶ - F - B♭ - B♭m⁶ - F - B♭ - B♭m⁶ - F

Exercise 31

We will use another two measure strum on this song. Play along with the Video to get the proper timing and feel.

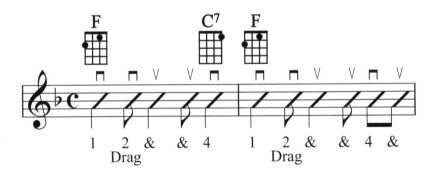

Combine these strums with the C, C⁷, F, F⁷, B♭, and B♭m⁶ chords to play a Calypso favorite, *Sloop John B.*

The Sloop John B.

Bahamian Folk Song

So hoist up the John B sails
See how the mainsail sets
Call for the captain ashore
Let me go home, let me go home
I wanna go home, yeah yeah
Well I feel so break up
I wanna go home

The first mate he got drunk
And broke in the captains trunk
The constable had to come and take him away
Sheriff John Stone
Why don't you leave me alone, yeah yeah
Well I feel so break up
I wanna go home

The B Chord

The Am Chord

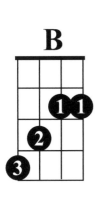

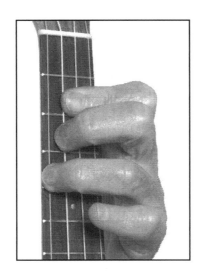

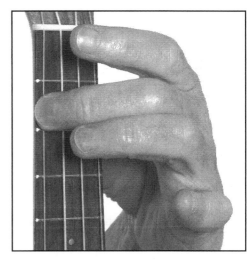

Exercise 32

Practice the following chord changes with the Em, B, and Am chords.

Em - B - Em - B - Em - B - Em - B - Em - B - Em - B - Em - B - Em

Em - Am - Em - Am - Em - Am - Em - Am - Em - Am - Em - Am - Em

The Reggae Strum

We'll use a **reggae** strum on this song. Play down up on 2 & and play up down on & 4. You'll be playing on 2 & & 4. Play along with the Video.

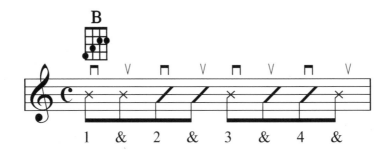

Combine the Em, B, and Am chords with the reggae strum to play *O Mary Don't You Weep*.

Use an electronic tuner to stay in good tune. They are inexpensive and user friendly.

O Mary Don't You Weep

Traditional

Mary wore three links of Chain
Every link was Jesus name.
Pharoah's army got drownded
O, Mary don't you weep
Chorus

One of these night about 12 o'clock
This old world is gonna rock.
Pharoah's army got drownded
O, Mary don't you weep
Chorus

37

In order to get a good muted strumming sound on this song, we need to play the C and C^7 chords in different positions.

The C Bar Chord

C

The C^7 Bar Chord

C^7

Exercise 33

Practice the following chord changes.

F - C - F - C - F - C - F - C - F - C - F - C - F - C - F - C - F - C

C - G - G^7 - C - G - G^7 - C - G - G^7 - C - G - G^7 -C - G - G^7

C - C^7 - F - C - C^7 - C - C^7 - F - C - C^7 - C - C^7 - F - C - C^7

Exercise 34

Here's a variation on the muted strum we used earlier.

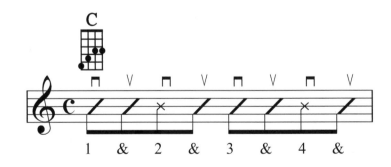

We'll use the C, C^7, F, G, & G^7 chords with this strum to play *Midnight Special.*

Midnight Special

Traditional

Let the Midnight Special shine a light on me
Let the Midnight Special shine a light on me
Let the Midnight Special shine a light on me
Let the Midnight Special shine an everloving light on me

Yonder comes Miss Rosie, how in the world did you know
By the way she wears her apron and the clothes she wore
Umbrella on her shoulder, piece of paper in her hand
She come to see the Governor, she wants to free her man

Chord Ornaments

Chord ornaments are notes that are added to chords to give them more variety and flavor and they can really spice up your playing. We'll use the first chord ornaments we study to play the 12 Bar Blues. See page 8 for a tablature explanation.

Exercise 35

Form the A chord (Position 1) and strum down up. Next, place your ring finger on the 3rd string @ 2nd fret (Position 2) and strum down up. Note that you will play down up on each position. We'll play 8 notes per measure - Position 1 - down up, Position 2 - down up, Position 1 - down up, Position 2 - down up. Play along with the Video. See page 8 for an explanation of ukulele tablature

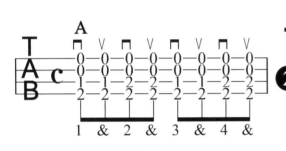

A Chord Position 1

A Chord Position 2

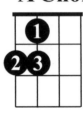

Exercise 36

Form the D chord (Position 1), using your index finger to bar across the 4th, 3rd, and 2nd string, and strum down up. Next, add your 2nd finger to the 2nd string @ 3rd fret (Position 2) and strum down up. As in the previous exercise, strum down up on each position. Play along with the Video.

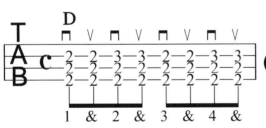

D Chord Position 1

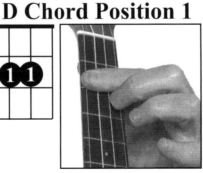

D Chord Position 2

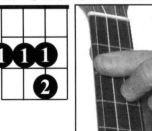

TIP *Practice should be fun. Only you can decide how much to practice and when. Everyone has their own limitations.*

Exercise 37

Form the E chord (Position 1) by moving the D chord up two frets to the 4th fret, and strum down up. Next, add your 2nd finger to the 2nd string @ 5th fret (Position 2) and strum down up. As in the previous exercise, strum down up on each position. Play along with the Video.

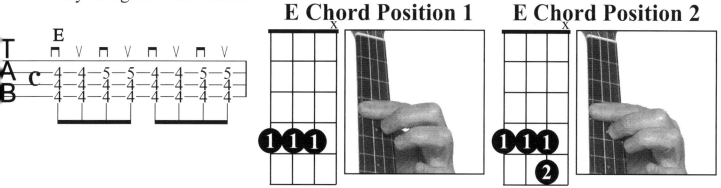

E Chord Position 1   E Chord Position 2

There are literally hundreds of songs that use the 12 Bar Blues chord progression. Using these three chord positions, we will play the *12 Bar Blues In A.* Play along with the Video.

12 Bar Blues in A

Traditional

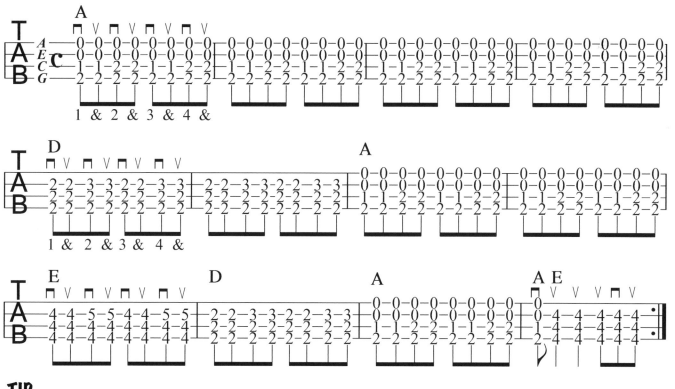

TIP
There are ukulele societies and organizations. Find one in your area and join.

You can also play the 12 Bar Blues in E using chord ornaments. We'll be using the E, A, and B chords.

Exercise 38

We've already learned the E and A positions, so let's start with the B position.

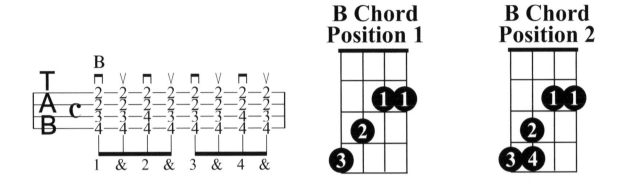

Now we'll use the E, A, and B position to play the *12 Bar Blues In E.* Play along with the Video.

12 Bar Blues in E

Traditional

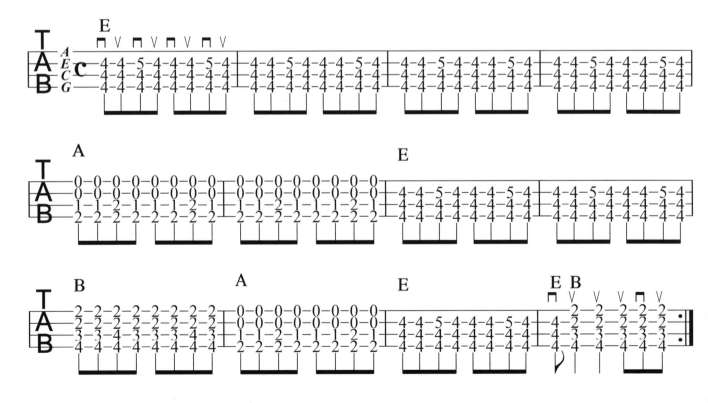

Appendix

You can watch the video at this address on the internet:

cvls.com/extras/ukulele/

If you encounter any issues with these files, please email us at
sales@cvls.com

Strum Library

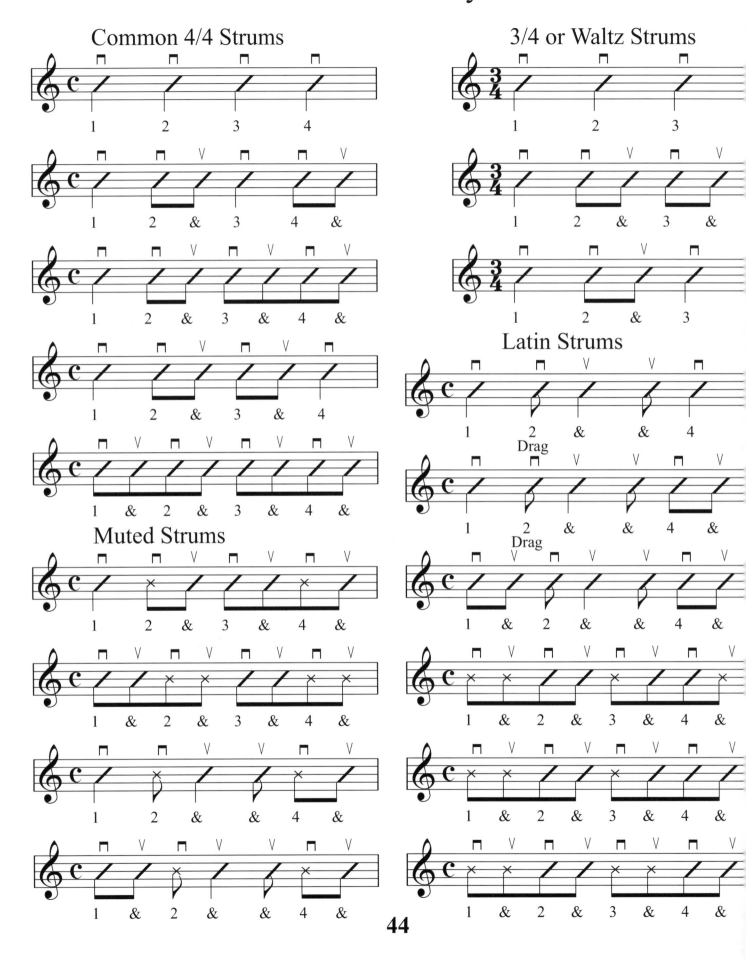

Ukulele for Guitar Players

For all you guitar players, there are similarities between the ukulele and guitar. The ukulele is tuned like the first four strings of a guitar with a capo on the 5th fret (G, C, A, E), with the exception being the 4th string of the ukulele is tuned an octave higher (G4 on the uke, G3 on the guitar).

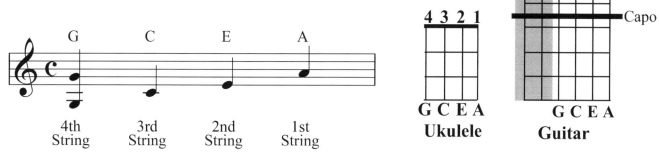

Playing the ukulele would be similar to playing a guitar with a capo at the 5th fret. You use the same chord shapes on the uke that you would on the guitar, taking into account that there are only four strings on the uke. If you're stumped on a ukulele chord and don't have a chord chart handy, count up to the 5th of the uke chord for the fingering on guitar. For example, a C chord on the uke is fingered like a G chord on the guitar capoed at the 5th fret (count up the alphabet C D E F G). A G chord on the uke is fingered like a D chord on the guitar capoed at the 5th fret (count G A B C D).

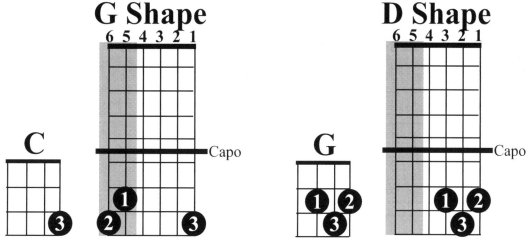

You can use most any guitar strum you know on the ukulele, as you can see from the previous page. You can also fingerpick a uke much like a guitar. You can even try to make up your own strums. There are also a lot of more advanced and unique ukulele strums that are beyond the scope of this course that were not covered here.

Music Theory

To become an accomplished ukulele player, you must understand some basic principals about the ukulele and music in general so that you can get the overall picture of the music you are playing.

A major scale consists of seven notes, which we will number 1-7.

Notes In Major Scales

Scale		1	2	3	4	5	6	7
Key of C		C	D	E	F	G	A	B
Key of G	(1♯)	G	A	B	C	D	E	F♯
Key of D	(2♯)	D	E	F♯	G	A	B	C♯
Key of A	(3♯)	A	B	C♯	D	E	F♯	G♯
Key of E	(4♯)	E	F♯	G♯	A	B	C♯	D♯
Key of F	(1♭)	F	G	A	B♭	C	D	E
Key of B♭	(2♭)	B♭	C	D	E♭	F	G	A
Key of E♭	(3♭)	E♭	F	G	A♭	B♭	C	D
Key of A♭	(4♭)	A♭	B♭	C	D♭	E♭	F	G

A **chromatic scale** consists of 12 notes, all the notes possible to play in one octave. All of the notes are shown below. The notes on top of each other are identical. For instance, the A♯ and the B♭ are the same. These are called **enharmonic tones**.

Chromatic Scale

1	2	3	4	5	6	7	8	9	10	11	12
A	A♯	B	C	C♯	D	D♯	E	F	F♯	G	G♯
	B♭			D♭		E♭			G♭		A♭

Notice that there is no note between B & C, and no note between E & F. A **half step** is one note in the chromatic scale (A to A♯ is a half step). This corresponds to one fret on the ukulele. A **whole step** is two notes in the chromatic scale (A to B is a whole step). This corresponds to two frets on the uke.

To figure out the notes in any major scale, use the following guides:

Notes	1	2	3	4	5	6	7	1
	whole step	whole step	half step	whole step	whole step	whole step	half step	

For example, to figure out the notes in an A scale, start with an A note in the chromatic scale. To go to note 2 make a whole step to B (2 frets on the ukulele). Note 3 would be a whole step to C♯. Note 4 is a half step to D (1 fret on the ukulele). Note 5 is a whole step to E. Note 6 is a whole step to F♯. Note 7 is a whole step to G♯. Note 1 is a half step back to A.

A relationship exists between scales and chords known as **chord progressions**. We started with several two and three chord songs. The most common chords used are the 1st, 4th, & 5th chords of a key. For example, we played in the key of G, using the G, C, & D chords. There are many songs that use only these three chords.

The following chart shows the common chord progressions that you will encounter:

Common Chords		Commonly Called	Example
1st	1st note of scale (major chord)	(Tonic)	G
4th	4th note of scale (major chord)	(Subdominant)	C
5th	5th note of scale (major chord)	(Dominant)	D
6th minor	6th note of scale (minor chord)	(Relative Minor)	Em
2nd	2nd note of scale (major chord)		A
2nd minor	2nd note of scale (minor chord)		Am
3rd	3rd note of scale (major chord)		B
3rd minor	3rd note of scale (minor chord)		Bm
$\flat$7th	7th note of scale moved down a half step (major chord)		F
1 (7th)	1st note of scale (dominant 7th chord) $1 \rightarrow 1$ (7th) $\rightarrow 4$		G^7
5 (7th)	5th note of scale (dominant 7th chord) $5 \rightarrow 5$ (7th) $\rightarrow 1$		D^7
$\flat$3rd	3rd note of scale moved down a half step (major chord)		$B\flat$
$\flat$6th	6th note of scale moved down a half step (major chord)		$E\flat$

A **major chord** consists of three notes, the 1st, 3rd, & 5th notes of that particular scale. Although we are strumming four strings at a time, we are only playing a combination of three notes. For example, the first chord we played was a C chord, which consists of C, E, & G. The 4 notes played when you strum a C chord are G, C, E, & C.

A **dominant 7th chord**, commonly called the 7th chord, is a four note chord consisting of the 1st, 3rd, 5th, & $\flat$7th notes of that scale. The 7th sound comes from adding the $\flat$7th note (7th lowered a half step). For example, a C7 chord is composed of C, E, G, & B$\flat$.

A **minor chord** consists of three notes, the 1st, $\flat$3rd, & 5th notes of that scale. The minor sound comes from lowering the 3rd a half step. A Cm chord is composed of C, E$\flat$, & G.

A **minor 7th chord** consists of the 1st, $\flat$3rd, 5th, & $\flat$7th notes of that scale. For example, a Cm^7 is composed of C, E$\flat$, G, & B$\flat$.

The following chart shows what notes are in these and other common chords:

Chord	Notes	Example	
Major	1st, 3rd, 5th	G	G, B, D
7th	1st, 3rd, 5th, $\flat$7th	G^7	G, B, D, F
Minor	1st, $\flat$3rd, 5th	Gm	G, B$\flat$, D
Minor 7th	1st, $\flat$3rd, 5th, $\flat$7th	Gm^7	G, B$\flat$, D, F
Major 7th	1st, 3rd, 5th, 7th	Gmaj^7	G, B, D, F$\sharp$
9th	1st, 2nd, 3rd, 5th, $\flat$7th	G^9	G, A, B, D, F
sus4	1st, 3rd, 4th, 5th	Gsus^4	G, B, C, D
Diminished	1st, $\flat$3rd, $\flat$5th	Gdim	G, B$\flat$, D$\flat$
Augmented	1st, 3rd, $\sharp$5th	G+	G, B, D$\sharp$

Chord Chart

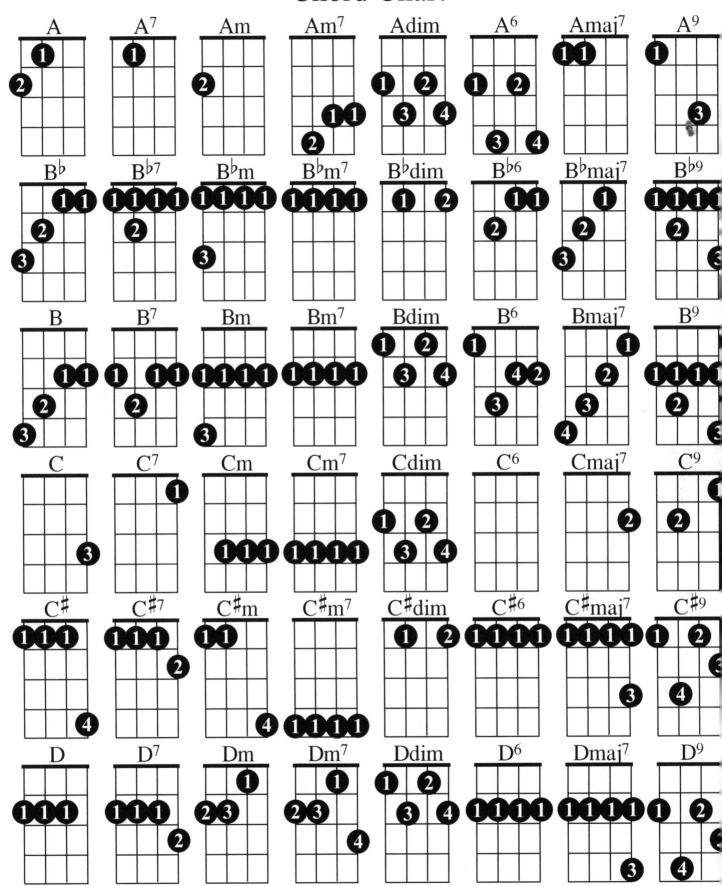

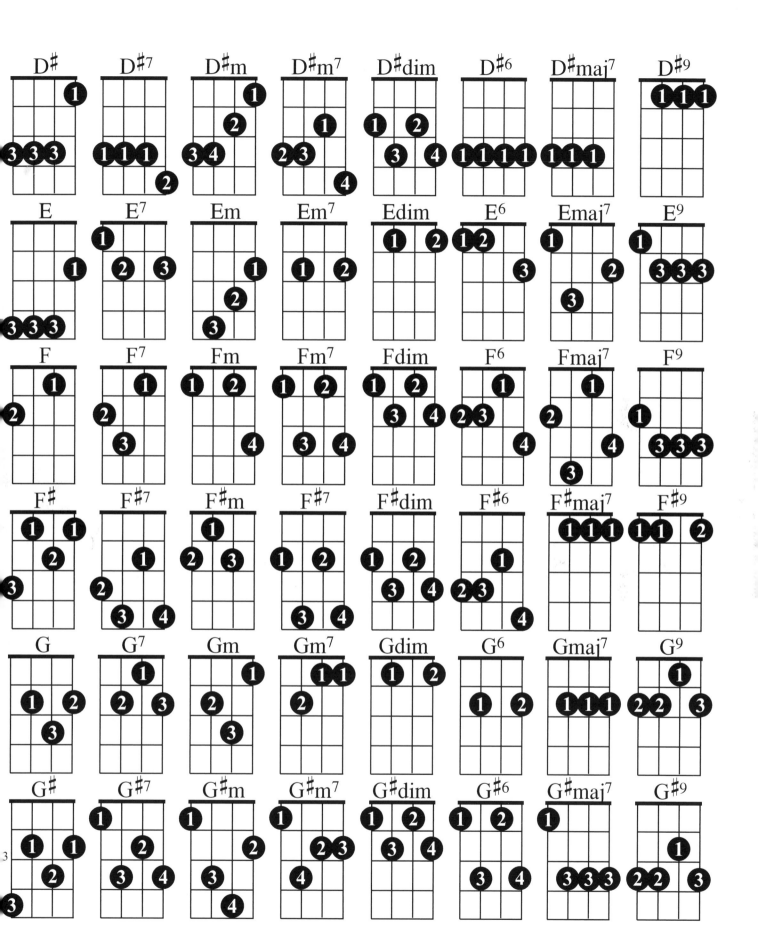

Made in the USA
Coppell, TX
02 August 2020